HAPPILY EVER CRAFTER

ONCE UPON A PIRATE CRAFT

ANNALEES LIM

Lerner Publications ◆ Minneapolis

First American edition published in 2020 by Lerner Publishing Group, Inc.

First published in Great Britain in 2018 by Wayland
Copyright © Hodder and Stoughton, 2018
All rights reserved.

Senior Commissioning Editor: Melanie Palmer
Design: Square and Circus
Illustrations: Supriya Sahai

Additional illustrations: Freepik

Lerner Publications Company
A division of Lerner Publishing Group, Inc.
241 First Avenue North
Minneapolis, MN 55401 USA

For reading levels and more information, look up this title at www.lernerbooks.com.

Main body text set in Billy Infant Regular 17/24.
Typeface provided by SparkyType.

Library of Congress Cataloging-in-Publication Data

Names: Lim, Annalees, author. | Sahai, Supriya, 1977- illustrator.
Title: Once upon a pirate craft / Annalees Lim, Supriya Sahai [illustrator].
Description: Minneapolis : Lerner Publications, [2018] | Series: Happily ever crafter | Audience: Ages 7–11. | Audience: Grades 4–6. | "First published in Great Britain in 2018 by Wayland."
Identifiers: LCCN 2018050537 (print) | LCCN 2018058681 (ebook) | ISBN 9781541561977 (eb pdf) | ISBN 9781541558786 (hb) | ISBN 9781526307149 (pb)
Subjects: LCSH: Handicraft—Juvenile literature. | Pirates—Juvenile literature. | Games—Juvenile literature. | Children's parties—Juvenile literature. | Handicraft for children.
Classification: LCC TT160 (ebook) | LCC TT160 .L48525 2019 (print) | DDC 745.5—dc23

LC record available at https://lccn.loc.gov/2018050537

Manufactured in the United States of America
1-46267-46259-11/26/2018

SAFETY INFORMATION:
Please ask an adult for help with any activities that could be tricky or involve cooking or handling glass. Ask adult permission when appropriate.

CONTENTS

ARGH M'HEARTIES!   4

DARING DRESS UP!   6

PIRATE PLANS   10

INVITATIONS   11

PARTY GAMES   12

PARTY DECORATIONS   17

PARTY FOOD   22

TREASURE TROVE   26

PIRATE PUZZLE   32

ARGH M'HEARTIES!

Come join us on a crafty adventure! You can create all the pirate-y things you need to be captain of the Seven Seas.

Pirates are well known for sailing the world's oceans and committing crimes along the way. They steal from ships and look for buried treasure on tropical islands dotted around the Seven Seas. The most famous pirates were from the Caribbean in the seventeenth and eighteenth centuries, but there were even pirates in Viking times—and some still exist today!

You won't need to spend all of your doubloons on expensive craft supplies—these crafts are made from things you can find around the house, using recycled materials or things you might have in your craft box. Follow the step-by-step instructions and you can impress your shipmates with your handmade costumes, decorations, gifts, and more!

FACT!
There is no evidence to suggest that pirates kept parrots as pets. It was first mentioned in the story *Treasure Island*, in which Long John Silver kept a pet parrot on his shoulder. Since then, parrots have been linked to pirates.

TOP TIP
Reusing unwanted things is a great way to make your craft project environmentally friendly. Always wash old food containers or fabric before you start using them. Don't forget to ask an adult before you take anything you see lying around the house—it might not be ready to be recycled just yet!

DARING DRESS UP!

Whether you need a costume for Halloween or for your very own costume party, you will find the perfect pirate project here. All of these costumes can be made without threading a single needle and can be made mostly from the recycled materials you have collected.

PIRATE HAT

Pirates were out in the open seas for weeks and months at a time, so a hat was important for keeping them cool from the sun. Make your own simple hat that will look great with the Pirate Crew outfit on page 9.

You Will Need:
- CARDSTOCK • MAGAZINES
- PAINT • PAINTBRUSH • SCISSORS
- TAPE • RULER

1. Cut out three identical hat shapes from the cardstock that are at least 14 inches long and 8 inches tall.

2. Use more cardstock to make a headband that is big enough to fit around your head.

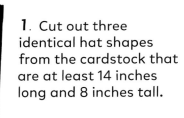

3. Staple the three shapes to the headband, then staple each shape together at the ends.

4. Paint the hat black and leave it to dry.

5. Decorate with a skull and crossbones made from the white paper. Attach some feathers made from colorful magazine pages.

SAILING SHIP

The typical ships of the 14th to 17th centuries were built to carry about forty people, but if they were stolen and became pirate ships the pirates would squeeze up to twice that number of people on board. Don't worry though. This costume is built just for one, so you will have plenty of room!

You Will Need:

- LARGE CARDBOARD BOX
- PAINT • PAINTBRUSH • FABRIC
- PLAIN T-SHIRT • NEWSPAPER
- TAPE • SCISSORS

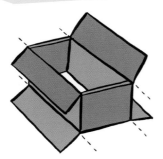

1. Cut off the top and bottom flaps of your box. Save these pieces for other craft projects.

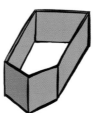

2. Make a crease at the front of the box so that it forms a point.

3. Paint the cardboard box to look like the ship's hull. Attach two long pieces of fabric to the cardboard with tape to make a pair of braces. These should be long enough so that you can put them over your shoulders.

4. Paint some sails and flags onto a plain T-shirt. Make sure you place some newspaper inside the T-shirt before you start to paint.

PIRATE HOOK

The most famous fictional pirate who had a hook for a hand is Captain James Hook from the book *Peter Pan* by J. M. Barrie. In the story, Hook loses his hand to a ferocious crocodile.

You Will Need:

- 2-LITER PLASTIC BOTTLE
- SCISSORS • TAPE • TIN FOIL
- GLUE • BLACK PAPER (OR MAGAZINE PAGES) • CARDSTOCK
- RULER • PENCIL

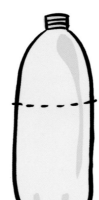

1. Cut the top 4 inches off the bottle and cover the edges with tape to cover any sharp edges.

2. Cut the cardstock so that it is 1 inch wide and longer than the width of the bottle.

3. Tape the cardstock strip across the inside of the bottle to make a handle.

4. Shape the foil into a hook and stuff it into the neck of the bottle. Tape in place.

5. Use glue to cover the base and glue on some torn-up pieces of black paper. Leave it to dry.

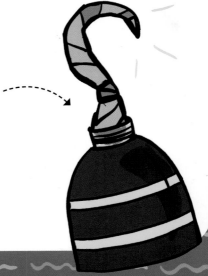

PIRATE CREW

There were many people on board pirate ships, all with different jobs. As well as sailors, there were cooks, surgeons, and even carpenters. Join the pirate gang by dressing up and you'll fit right in!

You Will Need:
- AN OLD T-SHIRT • SCISSORS
- MASKING TAPE • PAINT
- PAINTBRUSH • CONSTRUCTION PAPER • STRING • NEWSPAPER
- HOLE PUNCH

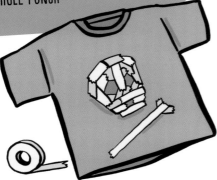

1. Use masking tape to create a skull and crossbones design on the front of the T-shirt.

2. Put the newspaper inside the T-shirt before painting two different colors of stripes onto the front. Leave it to dry before removing the masking tape and newspaper.

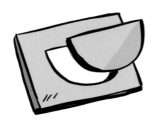

3. Draw a semi-circle shape onto some construction paper for the eyepatch and cut it out.

4. Punch a hole on either side of the eyepatch and paint it black.

DID YOU KNOW?

Many pirates wore stripes because they had spent time in prison or in the navy, both of which had stripy uniforms!

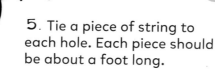

5. Tie a piece of string to each hole. Each piece should be about a foot long.

PIRATE PLANS

Planning a party is so much fun, especially when you have a great theme like pirates to base it around. You might be planning a party because it is your birthday, or you may want to throw a surprise party for your friends, or perhaps you just want to celebrate International Talk Like a Pirate Day on September 19!

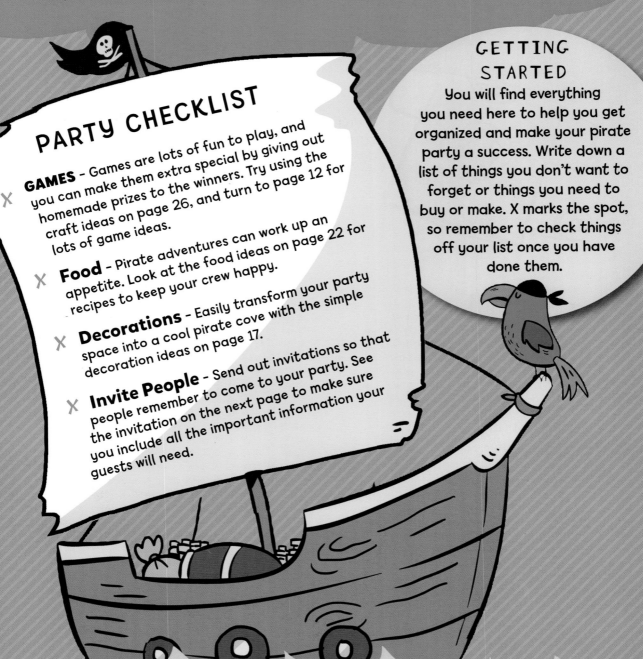

GETTING STARTED

You will find everything you need here to help you get organized and make your pirate party a success. Write down a list of things you don't want to forget or things you need to buy or make. X marks the spot, so remember to check things off your list once you have done them.

PARTY CHECKLIST

X **GAMES** - Games are lots of fun to play, and you can make them extra special by giving out homemade prizes to the winners. Try using the craft ideas on page 26, and turn to page 12 for lots of game ideas.

X **Food** - Pirate adventures can work up an appetite. Look at the food ideas on page 22 for recipes to keep your crew happy.

X **Decorations** - Easily transform your party space into a cool pirate cove with the simple decoration ideas on page 17.

X **Invite People** - Send out invitations so that people remember to come to your party. See the invitation on the next page to make sure you include all the important information your guests will need.

INVITATIONS

Write your invitations using this treasure map template. Make it extra special by rolling it up in an old plastic water bottle. Replace the lid with a cork to turn it into a secret message in a bottle.

Charter a course to: Say what kind of party your guests are invited to.

X marks the spot: State the address of where you are holding the party.

Ahoy there!: Write the name of the guest you are inviting.

AHOY THERE!

Charter a course to

Shiver me timbers!

Set sail

Date:

Time:

RSVP:

Shiver me timbers!: What kind of outfits do you want your guests to wear? Fancy, formal, or casual? You decide.

Set sail: Tell everyone when the party is happening.

RSVP: This means you would like your guests to tell you whether they can come. This helps you to plan how much food to make, how big the space needs to be, and how many goody bags to make.

PARTY GAMES

Lead your guests on fantastic pirate adventures with these exciting p-arrr-ty games. The fun doesn't just start when you begin to play. You will also enjoy making these games!

TREASURE HUNTERS

Pirates buried their stolen treasures in remote places, such as far-off desert islands. The only way they could find them again was to mark their location on a map with an X. Use this map to mark where you have hidden treasure and see whether your friends can find it!

You Will Need:

- PAPER • MARKERS • SCISSORS
- BOX WITH LID • GLUE STICK
- PLASTIC SHEET PROTECTOR
- BROWN PAPER • YELLOW PAPER

1. Draw a map of the space you're playing in. A yard or park works best for this game.

2. Place the map inside the plastic sheet protector.

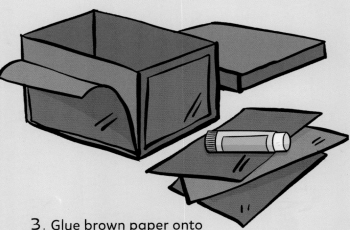

3. Glue brown paper onto all sides of the box using the glue stick.

HOW TO PLAY

Put candy or a toy inside the chest. Player 1 hides the treasure (while Players 2 and 3 don't look) and marks it on the map with an X using a dry-erase marker. Player 2 gets blindfolded and stands in the middle of the space. Player 3 uses the map to guide Player 2 to the treasure. Take turns until everyone has had a chance to find the treasure.

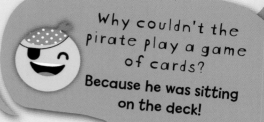

Why couldn't the pirate play a game of cards? Because he was sitting on the deck!

4. Attach yellow paper decorations to add the finishing touches.

5. Draw lines to make it look like a wooden treasure chest.

13

BURIED TREASURE

"Pieces of eight" were large Spanish coins made of silver that, because they were so popular, eventually became the first worldwide currency. Make your own coins for this game and see who can be the first to uncover the treasure.

You Will Need:

- ROUND CARDBOARD BOX
- TIN FOIL • GLUE STICK
- PERMANENT MARKER
- CUBE-SHAPED CARDBOARD BOX
- CONSTRUCTION PAPER • MARKERS
- SCISSORS • SAND

1. Cover the round box in tin foil and fix the foil in place using the glue stick.

2. Draw onto the coin using the pen. Remember, these coins usually had an "8" on them somewhere, so try hiding one in your design too.

3. Cover the cardboard cube with construction paper.

4. Decorate with a skull on every side. Draw either one or two bones underneath each skull. This will be your die for the game!

HOW TO PLAY

Fill a large plastic storage box with sand. Ask someone who isn't playing to bury the coin in the sand. Each player takes turns to roll the die. If it shows one bone, then the player can dig once in the sand. If it shows two bones, then they can dig twice. The first player to discover the coin is the winner.

MESSAGE IN A BOTTLE

People at sea often wrote messages, sealed them in a bottle, and then threw them into the ocean. There was no way to make them reach the people they were intended for, so they were often discovered years later in different places around the world.

You Will Need:
- 10 SMALL WATER BOTTLES WITH CAPS • PAPER • MARKERS
- SCISSORS • PLASTIC BAG
- WIRE COAT HANGER • STRING

1. Cut up ten pieces of paper that are just a bit shorter than the bottles.

2. Draw a star on one piece of paper and a skull and crossbones on the rest.

3. Roll up each piece of paper and tie it using the string to create a scroll. Put one scroll in each of the ten bottles.

4. Make a loop from a cut-up plastic bag and tie it around the neck of the bottle.

5. Bend a wire coat hanger so that it looks like a hook on a stick.

HOW TO PLAY
Fill a large plastic storage box with water and place the bottles inside. Everyone takes turns to hook a bottle and remove it from the water. The winner is the first person to find the bottle containing the scroll with the star.

WALK THE PLANK

As punishment, some pirates were told to walk down a plank of wood that extended out from the deck of a ship, often into shark-infested waters. Play this game to see who will survive and be crowned the captain of the ship!

You Will Need:
- MASKING TAPE • PAPER • MARKERS
- SCISSORS • A BLINDFOLD

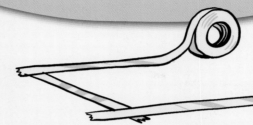

1. Use the masking tape to mark out a long plank shape in the middle of the room.

2. Draw a small island with a palm tree onto a piece of paper and cut it out.

3. Draw some sharks onto other pieces of paper and cut them out.

HOW TO PLAY

Blindfold the first player and spin them around three times. Stand them at one end of the plank. The winner is the player who walks down to the other end of the plank and makes it to the island without stepping into the shark-infested water.

FACT!
It was often thought that having women on a ship was bad luck, but this did not stop many adventurous women from becoming famous pirates.

4. Stick the sharks and island around the plank with the masking tape.

PARTY DECORATIONS

Give your party space a makeover and turn it into a desert island that will be the perfect paradise for pirates.

BARRELS

Pirates and those sailing around the world would need to take lots of supplies with them on their long adventures at sea. Their supplies would often be kept in wooden barrels and rolled onto the ship because they would have been too heavy to carry.

You Will Need:

- 2 PLASTIC BOTTLES • TAPE
- BROWN PAPER • GLUE
- GOLD CARDSTOCK • SCISSORS
- BLACK MARKER • GLUE STICK
- PAINTBRUSH

1. Cut the two bottles in half. You just need the bottoms for this craft. You can save the tops for the Hook craft on page 8.

2. Tape the two bottle bottoms together.

3. Glue some torn up brown pieces of paper all around the bottle and leave it to dry.

4. Cut two gold strips and glue them around the top and bottom.

5. Write your name or anything you want on the barrel.

TOP TIP

If you make six barrels, you could make them spell out P-I-R-A-T-E as a cool table decoration!

TREASURE CHEST

Arrange your bite-sized snacks in this treasure chest food display. Keep the lid closed to make sure your food stays fresh until you are ready to serve it to your guests.

1. Draw around the edges of your plastic food boat onto a piece of paper and cut it out.

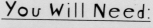

2. Use this as a template to draw the base, the sides of the chest, and the lid onto some cardstock.

3. Color the sides in with your markers to make them look like parts of a treasure chest. Draw planks, locks, and clasps.

4. Cut out the sides and tape them together.

5. Make sure the food boat fits inside the base before you tape the lid onto your base.

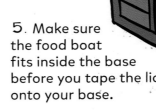

SKULL DANGLERS

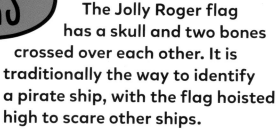

The Jolly Roger flag has a skull and two bones crossed over each other. It is traditionally the way to identify a pirate ship, with the flag hoisted high to scare other ships.

You Will Need:
- WHITE PAPER • PENCIL • SCISSORS
- STRING • GLUE STICK • MARKER

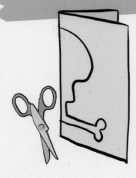

1. Draw a skull. Then fold the piece of paper in half. Cut it out and open it up.

2. Use this as a template to cut out five more identical skulls and fold them all in half.

3. Glue a loop of string in the middle of one of the folded shapes.

4. Glue the folded halves on top of each other.

5. Open up the glued stack and glue the two ends together to make a 3D shape. Draw a face on each.

TOP TIP Hang lots of danglers together on some string to make a cool decoration.

PALM TREES

Turn broken umbrellas into beautiful palm tree decorations that you can hang from the ceiling.

You Will Need:

- OLD UMBRELLA • GREEN AND BROWN CONSTRUCTION PAPER
- SCISSORS • TAPE

1. Remove the fabric from the wire using some scissors. You can put these scraps aside and save them for other craft projects.

2. Cut out lots of green leaves from green paper or magazines. You could also cut up old green plastic bags.

Why was the pirate ship so cheap to buy?

Because it was on sail!

3. Tape the leaf shapes onto the wires.

4. Cut up a long piece of brown paper. Or, you can tape lots of smaller scraps of paper together.

5. Tape one end of the brown paper to the top of the handle, wind it around the handle, and then fasten it to the bottom.

FACT!
Pirates didn't wear eyepatches because they were missing an eye from epic battles. They wore them to help their eyes adjust quickly to the darkness below deck, especially when they were raiding enemy ships.

TOP TIP
Tie some string to the top to hook the trees to the ceiling. Make several palm trees and hang them close together to make a shady canopy.

PARTY FOOD

Spoil your guests with these treasured treats. Some of these recipes need to be baked, so you will need the help of an adult. Remember to always wash your hands first!

GOLD COIN COOKIES

Gold coins were originally minted (or made) by hand. Unlike our coins today, they were imperfect and no two were alike!

You Will Need:

- 1 CUP OF BUTTER
- 1 CUP OF SUGAR
- 2 CUPS OF SELF-RISING FLOUR
- WHITE CHOCOLATE CHIPS
- ICING

1. Place the butter and sugar in a bowl and mix them together.

2. Add the flour and chocolate chips and mix by hand until it forms a dough.

10-15 MINUTES!

3. Roll the dough into balls and flatten them out onto a baking tray.

TOP TIP

You can always decorate pre-made cookies. This is a great activity for you and your pirate party guests to do together.

4. Bake the cookies for 10-15 minutes on a medium heat, or until they are golden brown.

5. Once they have cooled, decorate them with the icing.

DESERT ISLAND PUNCH

You Will Need:
- CLEAN POLYSTYRENE PIZZA BASE
- BOWL • WHITE CHOCOLATE
- CEREAL • GREEN FOOD DYE
- CHOCOLATE FINGER COOKIE
- WAX PAPER • SPOON

This delicious fruity recipe is simple to make but packs a real punch—and everyone will love the special way it is served.

1. Cut the pizza base into an oval.

2. Melt some white chocolate in a bowl and add a few drops of green food dye. Pour some of the chocolate into leaf shapes on a sheet of wax paper and leave it to set.

Stick the chocolate finger cookie in the middle of the mixture.

3. Melt more white chocolate in a bowl and pour in some cereal. Mix well.

4. Sculpt a lump of the white chocolate mixture in the middle of the base.

5. Unpeel the leaves and glue them onto the chocolate finger using more melted chocolate.

PUNCH RECIPE
Crush some blueberries and blackberries together in the bottom of a bowl. Add some lemonade and mix well. Add some cut-up fruit and ice cubes. Place the floating desert island on top before serving.

GEMS AND JEWELS GELATIN

This fun, multicolored dessert tastes great and can be served in so many different ways. Place it in a bowl and add whipped cream, top it with scoops of ice cream, or eat it with lots of fruit.

1. Make three different flavors of gelatin and leave them to set.

2. Cut them up into small pieces and mix together in a big bowl.

3. Pour the chopped pieces into ice trays.

4. Make another flavor of gelatin and pour it into the ice trays. Leave it to set.

5. Turn the tray over and tap lightly to remove the gelatin from the mold. If the pieces are stuck, dip the bottom of the tray in some warm water first.

SHIP'S WHEEL PIZZA

A ship's wheel is attached to the rudder and steers the boat. It's made from hardwood, which is less likely to be damaged from the salt in seawater. The wheel is usually made up of eight spokes.

You Will Need:
- PIZZA DOUGH • CHEESE
- BUTTER • GARLIC • SALT AND PEPPER • KNIFE • ROLLING PIN

1. Roll the pizza dough out into a circle that is about 1 inch thick.

2. Ask an adult to cut a star shape in the middle of the dough using the knife.

3. Place some cheese on the edge and cover it with a triangle of dough. Press down so that none of the cheese escapes when it melts.

4. Repeat with the rest of the triangles to complete the wheel.

TOP TIP
Serve the pizza with a bowl of BBQ sauce in the middle of the wheel.

5. Melt the butter and add some chopped garlic, salt, and pepper. Spread over the wheel. Bake for 15–20 minutes or until golden brown.

25

TREASURE TROVE

Transform old junk into treasures with these pirate crafts. Make them to add to the party decorations found on page 17, as prizes for the games you play, or just because crafting is so much fun!

TELESCOPE

Sailors used to navigate the seas using the stars in the night sky, so telescopes were an essential tool for any pirate.

You Will Need:
- CARDSTOCK • PAPER CUP
- PLASTIC SHEET PROTECTOR
- TAPE • SCISSORS • PAINT
- PAINTBRUSH • GLUE STICK
- PENCIL

1. Roll up the cardstock into a tube and tape in place. Make it the same size as the bottom of the paper cup.

2. Cut off the bottom of the cup and tape the tube to the hole.

3. Draw around the top of the cup, then draw another circle slightly bigger than it to make a ring.

4. Cut the ring shape out. Glue some plastic onto the ring and then glue this onto the end of the cup.

5. Paint the telescope and leave it to dry before you use it.

TOP TIP
Draw a desert island scene onto the plastic so you can see it every time you look through the telescope.

SHIP'S RAT

Ship's rat is another name for the black rat. It was found on board many of the boats that sailed the seas. They moved fast and loved to climb, but most of the time they were looking for food that was stored in the wooden barrels inside the ship.

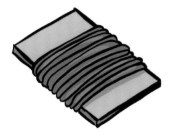

1. Wrap yarn around a piece of square cardboard.

2. Bend the cardboard slightly so that it creates a gap and carefully remove the cardboard, keeping the yarn as straight as possible.

You Will Need:
- YARN • CARDBOARD • SCISSORS
- FABRIC SCRAPS (OR FELT)
- FABRIC GLUE

3. Wrap a long piece of yarn around the middle and tie it tightly together to make a pom-pom.

4. Trim the pom-poms if necessary using scissors. Repeat so you have two pom-poms in total.

5. Cut out ears, a nose, feet, and a tail from felt or fabric scraps.

SQUEAK!

What shivers at the bottom of the ocean?

A nervous wreck!

6. Glue the two pom-poms together and decorate them with the ears, nose, feet, and tail.

SHIPWRECK

The seas were once very dangerous places with lots of cannons firing at enemy boats. If a boat sank, its treasures usually sank with it. Lots of people still search for shipwrecks and their hidden treasures today, but you can make your very own ship on which to store your treasures.

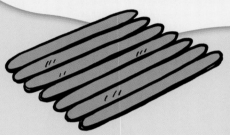

1. Line up some popsicle sticks together so that they make a square.

You Will Need:
- POPSICLE STICKS
- COCKTAIL SKEWERS
- GLUE • THREAD
- MODELING CLAY • SCISSORS

2. Glue two more sticks on top to attach the sticks together. You may need to trim them to size first.

3. Turn this over and build up the sides, gluing each layer in place until the sides are about 2 inches tall.

4. Use thread to make a cocktail skewer mast.

5. Roll the modeling clay into a ball and use it to stick the mast in place.

CANNON

Cannons were popular weapons for boats, as they could be fired far and cause lots of damage. Gunpowder was lit at one end and the explosion would cause the cannonball to be pushed out of the barrel with great force.

You Will Need:
- PAPER TOWEL TUBE • BLACK PAINT
- BROWN MARKERS • PAINTBRUSH
- BLACK PAPER • 2 BRASS FASTENERS
- SCISSORS • CARDSTOCK

1. Cut up the tube so you have one longer piece and four small rings.

2. Paint all of these pieces black and leave them to dry.

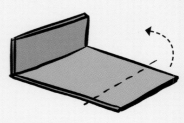

3. Make a square "U" shape from the cardstock and paint it to look like wood.

4. Use brass fasteners to attach the tube to the cardstock. This lets you aim your cannon.

5. Glue the four rings to the sides to make the wheels. You can decorate these by gluing paper spokes to the outside of the rings.

PIRATE PARROT

Brightly colored macaws were valuable pets. Pirates often took them to sell in countries like the United States. They were easy to transport since they were small and could be taught to repeat words or songs, making the long sea journeys much more fun!

You Will Need:
- BRIGHTLY COLORED SOCK
- WOOL • FABRIC GLUE • SCISSORS
- CARDBOARD • FABRIC SCRAPS

1. Fill half of one sock with fabric scraps and tie the open end with some wool.

2. Cut the tied end with scissors to make a feathery tail.

3. Make some feet from cardboard and glue the stuffed sock to this using fabric glue. Leave it to dry while you make the rest of the decorations.

4. Cut out a triangle, two small circles, and two wing shapes. Glue these to the sock using more fabric glue.

PIECES OF EIGHT!

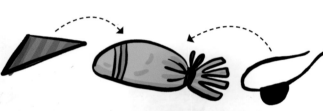

5. Make a headscarf and eyepatch from more fabric scraps and tie them onto the sock parrot.

OCTOPUS WINDOW STICKER

Decorate your window to make a pirate's paradise. Start by making this simple octopus design and then choose what you would like to add next. Make sunken treasures, shipwrecks, or even schools of tropical fish.

1. Draw your octopus design onto a piece of paper and then put it inside the plastic sheet protector.

You Will Need:
- GLUE • GREEN FOOD COLORING
- DISH SOAP • PAINTBRUSH
- PLASTIC SHEET PROTECTOR
- BLACK PERMANENT MARKER
- PAPER • PENCIL

2. Mix together 1 tablespoon of glue with a drop of dish soap and a drop of food coloring. Stir until the streaks disappear.

3. Use the paintbrush to trace the design of the octopus directly onto the plastic. Make sure the layer of paint mixture is thick.

24 HOURS!

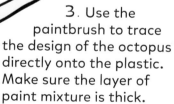

4. Leave it to dry in a warm place for at least 24 hours before you draw the details on using the black marker.

5. Peel off the plastic and place it on the window—it will stick all by itself!

PIRATE PUZZLE

CAN YOU FIND THE ANSWERS TO THESE QUESTIONS?

1. Which ship has discovered treasure?

2. How many fish are there?

3. Where is the parrot hiding?

4. Which ship has the most flags?

ANSWERS: 1.D 2.7 3.B 4.C